Finding Shapes

Rectangles

Diyan Leake

www.raintreepublishers.co.uk

Visit our website to find out more information about **Raintree** books.

To order:

☎ Phone 44 (0) 1865 888112

📄 Send a fax to 44 (0) 1865 314091

💻 Visit the Raintree Bookshop at **www.raintreepublishers.co.uk** to browse our catalogue and order online.

First published in Great Britain by Raintree, Halley Court, Jordan Hill, Oxford OX2 8EJ, part of Harcourt Education.
Raintree is a registered trademark of Harcourt Education Ltd.

Editorial: Diyan Leake
Design: Jo Hinton-Malivoire
Picture research: Maria Joannou
Production: Victoria Fitzgerald
Originated by Dot Gradations Ltd, UK
Printed and bound in China by South China Printing Company

10 digit ISBN 1 844 21332 3 (HB)
13 digit ISBN 978 1844 21332 0 (HB)
10 09 08 07 06
10 9 8 7 6 5 4 3 2 1

10 digit ISBN 1 844 21348 X (PB)
13 digit ISBN 978 1844 21348 1 (PB)
10 09 08 07
10 9 8 7 6 5 4 3 2 1

British Library Cataloguing in Publication Data
Leake, Diyan
516.1'5
Finding Shapes: Rectangles
A full catalogue record for this book is available from the British Library.

Acknowledgements
The publishers would like to thank the following for permission to reproduce photographs: Alamy pp. **13** (Rick Yamada-Lapides), **15** (Nic Cleave Photography), **17** (britishcolumbiaphotos.com); Corbis pp. **12** (McIntyre Photography), **14** (Abbie Enock); Getty Images pp. **5** (Stone/Erik

The author and publisher would like to thank Patti Barber, specialist in Early Years Education, University of London Institute of Education, for her advice and assistance in the preparation of this book.

The paper used to print this book comes from sustainable resources.

Contents

Some words are shown in bold, **like this**. They are explained in the glossary on page 23.

What is a rectangle?

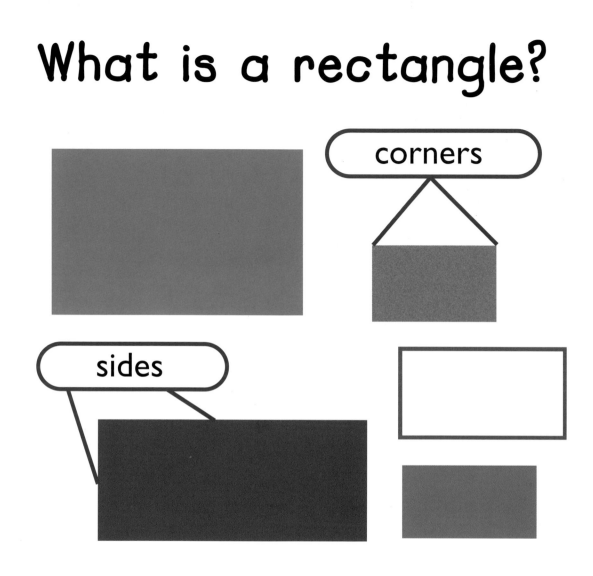

corners

sides

A rectangle is a **flat** shape with four **corners**.

You can see flat shapes but you cannot pick them up.

Rectangles have four **straight sides**.

The opposite sides of a rectangle are always the same length.

Can I see rectangles at home?

There are lots of rectangles at home.

Some of them are in the living room.

Cards can be rectangles.

What other rectangles are there at home?

There are rectangles in
the bedroom.

The front of each drawer is
a rectangle.

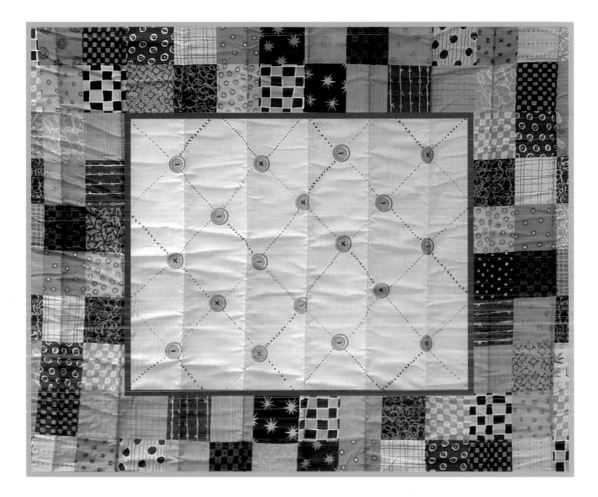

This quilt has a white rectangle
on it.

Can I see rectangles at school?

There are lots of rectangles at school.

Blackboards and whiteboards are rectangles.

This wall of bricks has rectangles on it.

Some rectangles are long and some are short.

Are there rectangles outside?

Some buildings have rectangles on the outside.

This brick school building has lots of rectangles.

You can see rectangles on a climbing frame.

This climbing frame is purple and yellow.

Are there rectangles in town?

We can see all sorts of rectangles in town.

The windows on these buildings are rectangles.

There are rectangles in car parks.

Each rectangle is the space for one car.

Are there rectangles in the countryside?

Fields in the countryside can be rectangles.

Farmers grow **crops** in the fields.

These hay bales are in a field.

Each **flat face** of the bales is a rectangle.

Can I see rectangles on other shapes?

faces

Rectangles can be part of a shape called a **cuboid**.

Each face on a cuboid is a rectangle.

You can stack cuboids on top of each other.

Have you ever seen a **hollow** cuboid?

A box is a **hollow cuboid**.

If something is hollow, you can put things in it.

People give presents in boxes.

This teddy will be a nice present.

What can I make with rectangles?

Make a pattern with rectangles of different colours!

Glossary

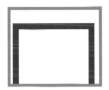
corners
parts of a shape where the sides come together

crops
plants that farmers grow in fields for food

cuboid
solid shape with six flat faces

flat
has no thickness to it

hollow
has space inside

sides
the outside lines of a flat shape

straight
not bent or curved

Index

Note to parents and teachers

Reading non-fiction texts for information is an important part of a child's literacy development. Readers can be encouraged to ask simple questions and then use the text to find the answers. Each chapter in this book begins with a question. Read the questions together. Look at the pictures. Talk about what the answer might be. Then read the text to find out if your predictions were correct. To develop readers' enquiry skills, encourage them to think of other questions they might ask about the topic. Discuss where you could find the answers. Assist children in using the contents page, picture glossary, and index to practise research skills and new vocabulary.